PAPERWHITE

USERS MANUAL

**The Ultimate Kindle Paperwhite Guide to Getting Started,
Advanced Tips and Tricks, and
Finding Unlimited Free Books**

By Steve Weber

Published by Stephen W. Weber
Printed in the United States of America
Weber Books   www.WeberBooks.com
ISBN: 978-1-936560-19-6

Free Kindle books, all you can eat!

Kindle Buffet is a daily website that features a hand-picked list of great Kindle books being offered free that day. Includes mysteries, romance, science-fiction, horror, non-fiction and more. Today's bestsellers and yesterday's classics. You may never need to pay for a book again! See for yourself by visiting www.KindleBuffet.com

Allison (A Kane Novel)

Mystery, Thriller & Suspense
Author: Steve Gannon

Allison Kane, a journalism student at UCLA, takes a summer job as a TV news intern—soon becoming involved in a scandalous murder investigation and the media firestorm that follows—a position that pits her squarely against her iron-fisted police detective father.

Cafenova (Clairmont Series)

Christian Fiction > Romance
Author: S. Jane Scheyder

Leaving her broken heart behind in Seattle, Maddy Jacobs starts a new life on the coast of Maine. Although running a Bed and Breakfast has always been her dream, restoring the sprawling Victorian inn is a massive undertaking. Her contractor, competent, handsome, and built like a Greek god, could be the answer to her prayers. If she can keep her wits about her, she might just survive the summer.

20 Things I've Learned as an Entrepreneur

Small Business & Entrepreneurship
Author: Alicia Morga

20 Things I've Learned as an Entrepreneur is the summary of lessons leading female technology entrepreneur Alicia Morga learned as a first-time entrepreneur in Silicon Valley. If you're an entrepreneur or if you've only dreamed about starting your own business, this quick important read is for you.

Contents

Introduction

The revolutionary Amazon Paperwhite

Beyond the shadow of a doubt, Amazon's latest-generation Kindle Paperwhite offers the best digital reading experience available today. It's simply no contest. When you consider the quality of the hardware plus the richness of Amazon's unsurpassed library of content, it's an unbeatable combination. Nothing else even comes close, and nothing can threaten the Paperwhite's dominance for the foreseeable future.

The Paperwhite is the perfect e-reader, whether you're sitting on the beach or reclined in bed. With no glare in bright sunlight, and the built-in backlight, you can read for hours on end with no eyestrain whatsoever, and no worrying about battery stamina. Lighter in weight than most small paperbacks, the Paperwhite allows you to concentrate on reading, without distractions like email.

But reading text is only the beginning. The built-in dictionary provides quick access to definitions, and its link to Wikipedia and the X-Ray feature provide instant explanations of characters, settings, and more. You can read the complete text of footnotes without losing your place. There are no confusing buttons.

The Paperwhite comfortably carries up to 1,100 books in your back pocket or purse.

Everything is handled by the intuitive touchscreen interface.

And, of course, the Paperwhite can hold a huge library of your favorite books—up to 1,100—and instant access to new books. The Whispersync feature syncronizes your last-read location, bookmarks, and annotations across all your devices—other Kindles and Kindle apps available for smartphones and computers.

You have access to more than a million titles priced at $4.99 and less, not to mention a treasure trove of newspapers and magazines. And at participating public libraries, you can borrow Kindle books at no charge, and you don't even have to visit the library. You can lend your Kindle books to other Kindle users for up to two weeks.

If you should lose your Kindle, no worries—your entire library is backed up at no charge in Amazon's "Cloud" wireless storage

Read in direct sunlight with no glare, no eyestrain.

The Paperwhite is the official e-reader of the National PTA.

system. Never worry about misplacing or losing a book again.

You can also use your Kindle to view personal documents. You can email Word, PDF and other documents directly to your Kindle and read them in Kindle format.

The Paperwhite is invaluable for the whole family. You can encourage kids' love of reading with thousands of free classics like *Alice in Wonderland*, *Black Beauty*, *Peter Pan*, and *Treasure Island*. With Kindle FreeTime, you can encourage your kids to read even more, with all-you-can-eat access to great books, while you receive progress reports on the total time spent reading and number of words looked up. With the built-in Vocabulary Builder, kids can quiz themselves with flashcards to strengthen their word retention.

The Paperwhite supports illustrated children's books, too, with pop-up text and Panel View, allowing them to read comic books panel by panel.

You can organize your library into customized collections, or categories, to easily access any book you're searching for.

You can customize the Paperwhite for use in English, Spanish, Brazilian Portuguese, French, German, Italian, Japanese, and Simplified Chinese. Simply select the language you're most comfortable with, and enjoy instant dictionary lookups in any of these languages.

Of course, you'll receive personalized recommendations from Amazon for great new books, right on your device. Offers are displayed on the screensaver and the bottom of the home screen while you're not using your device.

1 ► FAST START GUIDE

Your Kindle Paperwhite will be partially charged when you take it out of the box. You can charge the battery with the supplied USB cable, connected to a computer. Fully charging the battery normally takes four to six hours.

To charge your device without a computer, you'll need to purchase a compatible wall adapter for the USB cable.

Charging Your Paperwhite

TIP: To conserve battery life, place your Kindle into sleep mode after you're finished using it. Press and release the power button to put your device in sleep mode.

When your device is charging, a **lightning bolt** appears on the battery icon at the top of the **Home** screen. While your Kindle is charging, the charge indicator light glows amber. When your device is fully charged, the indicator light glows green.

When you connect your device to a computer, the screen will indicate the device is in "USB Drive Mode."

You can use your Paperwhite while it's connected to the computer if you "eject" the device from your computer so that it exits USB Drive Mode.

- **For Windows computers:** Click on My Computer, then right-click on your Kindle.

- **For Macs:** Click the Eject button beside the Kindle in any Finder window, or drag the Kindle from the Desktop to the Trash.

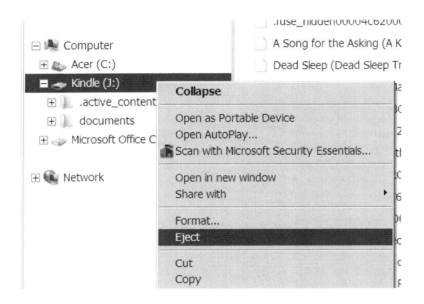

At left: On your computer, right-click on the Kindle to safely eject the device from USB Drive Mode. Now you can use the device while connected—or safely disconnect the device from your computer.

Registering Your Paperwhite

If you purchased your Kindle Paperwhite yourself, it should be delivered already set up and connected to your Amazon account. In case you received the device as a gift, or it's not registered to your Amazon account, here is the registration procedure:

1. From the **Home** screen tap the **Menu** ☰ icon, then tap **Settings**.

2. Tap Registration.

3. Choose the Amazon account you want to use with your Paperwhite.

   - **If you already have an Amazon account:** Tap this option. Enter your Amazon email address and password. Tap **Register**. When finished, your name will appear as the Registered User.

   - **If you don't have an Amazon account:** Tap this option and follow the instruction on the screen to set up a new Amazon account.

Basic Navigation

You'll need just a few basic controls to use your Paperwhite. Turn on the device by pressing the power button on the bottom of the device.

To turn off your device, press and hold the power button for seven seconds.

After a few minutes of inactivity, your device will enter sleep mode to conserve power. A screen saver will be displayed, which requires no power. Press the power button to awaken your Paperwhite, and swipe your finger across the bottom of the screen to begin using the device.

Navigating the Home Screen

The **Home** screen, pictured below, shows a list of the content stored on your Paperwhite. Here you can manage and organize your Kindle books and other content.

To go to the **Home** screen, tap the **Home** 🏠 icon. (If the **Home** icon isn't visible, tap the top of your screen, and the **Home** icon appears in the toolbar.)

Near the top left corner of the **Home** screen, there's a tab for **On Device** and another tab for **Cloud**.

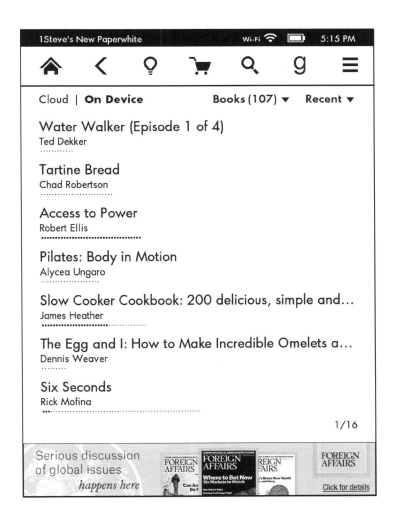

At left: The Paperwhite Home screen in "List View," which shows the titles stored on the device. An alternate view, "Cover View," shows the cover images of the books.

It looks It looks like the illustration above.

- **Open a book:** Tap the **On Device** tab to view the items downloaded to your device. Tap a title to open it.

- **Remove a book:** Press and hold the title, then tap **Remove from Device**. The title is erased from your Paperwhite and added to the **Cloud** tab, where it's available for downloading again.

- **Sort books and other items:** You can view your list of titles sorted by **Recent**, **Title**, **Author** or **Collections**.

- **Filter by type of document:** Tap **My Items**, then tap **All Items**, **Books**, **Periodicals**, **Docs**, or **Active Content**.

- **Search for a book or periodical:** Tap the **Magnifying Glass** icon in the toolbar. Tap **My Items** to search your library. Or widen your search to include the **Kindle Store**, **Dictionary**, or **Wikipedia**.

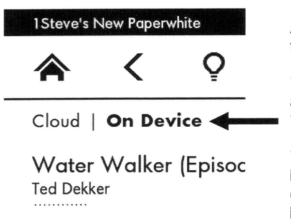

At left: A view of the top left corner of the Paperwhite Home screen.

The "On Device" tab shows items already downloaded to your Kindle. Tap an item to open it.

Tap on the "Cloud" tab to view all items, including those not yet downloaded to your Paperwhite. Tap an item to download it to your device.

Navigating With the Touchscreen Interface

Just as you'd do with a paperback book, the Paperwhite allows you to easily turn pages in a Kindle book. Tapping almost anywhere on the display area will bring you to the following page. Tap the left side of the screen to return to the previous page.

The touchscreen navigation works whether you're holding your Paperwhite in **Portrait Mode** (like a small paperback) or in **Landscape Mode** (like a coffee-table book).

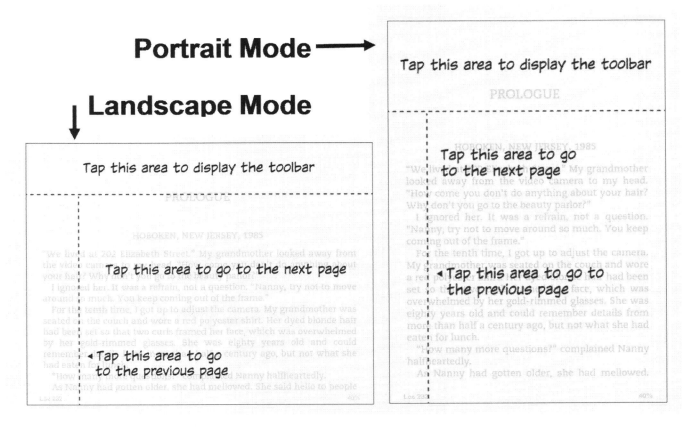

An alternate way to navigate pages is by swiping the screen with your finger. To advance to the next page, swipe your finger across the screen from the right to left. To return to the previous page, swipe your finger from left to right.

To select an item, simply tap it. For example, tap a book cover or title on your **Home** screen to open the book.

To switch between **Portrait** mode and **Landscape** mode:

1. While reading, tap the top of the screen to reveal the **Reading Toolbar**.

2. Tap the **Menu** ≡ icon, then tap **Landscape** mode (or **Portrait m**ode).

Navigating Comics and Graphic Novels

Some graphic novels and comics are specially formatted for viewing on Kindles, supporting features such as **Kindle Panel View**, **Kindle Text Pop-Up**, and zooming in on and panning across images and tables.

*   View one panel at a time:

1. Double-tap the page to launch **Panel View**.

2. Tap the right side of the screen to advance to the next panel. Tap the left side of the screen to view the previous panel.

3. Double-tap the panel to exit **Panel View**.

- Zoom in or pan across images and tables:

1. Double-tap the image or table.

2. Pinch outward to zoom in, or press and drag to pan across the image or table.

3. Pinch inward to zoom out, or tap the **X** in the upper-right corner of the image to continue reading.

Navigating with Toolbars

Depending on what content you're viewing at the moment, you can access three navigation toolbars—the **standard** toolbar, **reading** toolbar, and **reading navigation** toolbar.

Tap the top of your screen to display a toolbar. Below is a picture of the **Standard** toolbar.

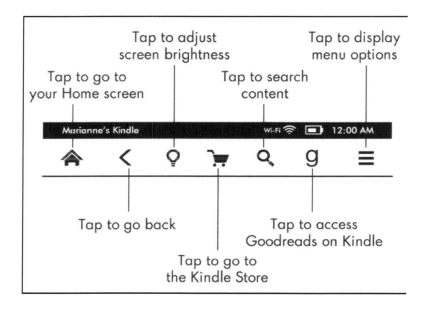

At left: The Standard toolbar appears at the top of the screen when you click the "Home" icon.

The options which appear in the **Standard** toolbar are:

Home: Tap 🏠 to go to the **Home** screen, where you'll see a list of the books and other content stored on your Paperwhite.

Back: Tap ❮ to retrace your steps. For example, if you tap a link in the book and the web page opens, tap **Back** to return to the book.

Brightness : Tap 💡 to adjust the brightness of your display.

Kindle Store: The cart 🛒 icon links to Amazon's Kindle bookstore. You must have a wireless connection to access the store.

Search: Tap the **magnifying glass** 🔍 icon to display a search box, enabling you to search your books.

Goodreads: The **Goodreads** g icon provides access to Goodreads, a community for book lovers where you can rate and share book recommendations.

Menu: The **menu** ≡ icon displays a list of options including the **Kindle store**, **View special offers**, **sync and check for items**, and **Settings**.

While you're reading a book, if you tap the top of the screen, the **Reading** toolbar is displayed, as pictured below:

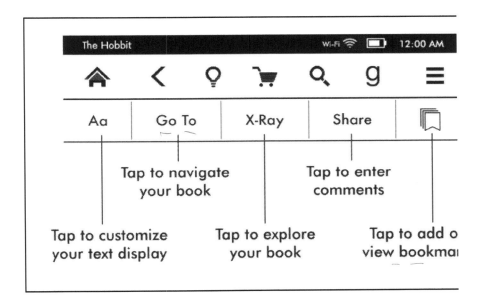

At left: The Reading toolbar appears when you tap the top of the screen while reading a document.

The Reading Toolbar options include:

Text (Aa): Tap to display font and text options. Adjust the font size, typeface, publisher font, line spacing, and margins.

Go To: Opens navigation tabs including **Contents** (show chapter headings) and **Notes** (to view your notes and highlights, and public notes and highlights).

X-Ray: Explore the book's "skeleton." You'll see all passages in a book mentioning specific ideas, characters, historical figures, places or topics. If X-Ray isn't enabled for the book you're viewing, the button is disabled.

Share: Tap to share your thoughts with other readers.

Bookmark: Add or delete a bookmark on the current page. View prevously added bookmarks.

When reading, swipe up from the bottom of the page to display the **reading navigation** toolbar, which provides a graphic illustration of your progress in a book and lets you quickly jump ahead to preview upcoming sections. The toolbar is pictured below:

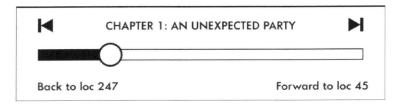

Above: The reading navigation toolbar gives a visual indication of how far along in a document you are.

Periodical Toolbar

When you're reading a magazine or newspaper, you'll see a special toolbar when you tap the top of the screen.

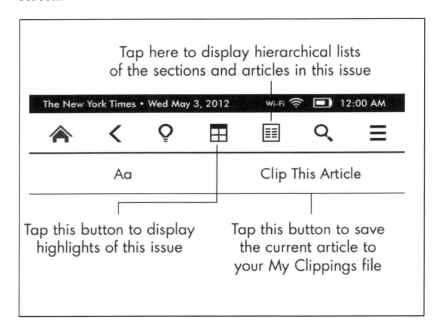

At left: The Periodical toolbar appears when you tap the top of the screen while reading a newspaper or magazine.

Periodical Home: Tap to display highlights of the issue you're reading.

Sections and Articles: Tap to see a hierarchical list of sections and articles.

Another toolbar is available for periodicals on the article detail page. The options are:

Text (Aa): Tap to display font and text options.

Clip This Article: Tap to clip an article to your **My Clippings** file. The file, located on your **Home** screen, stores your notes, bookmarks, highlights, and clipped articles.

Using the On-screen Keyboard

When you tap the **Search** 🔍 icon or initiate other actions requiring you to type text, the on-screen keyboard appears at the bottom of the screen, as shown below.

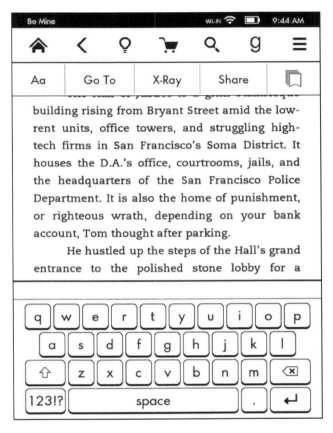

At left: The on-screen keyboard appears when you're required to enter text.

To enter numbers or symbols, tap the **numbers** key 123!?. Tap the **ABC** key to return to the regular keyboard. Tap the shift key ⇧ to enter capital letters.

If you have a smartphone or other touch-screen device, you're probably already familiar with the basics of a touch-screen keyboard. If you're not, the learning curve shouldn't be too steep, but there may be some frustration initially. Here are some basic tips to keep in mind.

- It's easier to type accurately if your Paperwhite is in landscape mode—the keyboard is enlarged, giving you more room to type.

- Use your thumbs to type while holding the device in your hand.

Viewing Status Indicators

Along the top of your **Home** screen, you'll see indicators to the status of your Paperwhite. You can also view these indicators within a book by tapping the top of the screen to display the toolbar.

The first three indicators we'll look at are **wireless** status indicators:

Wi-Fi 🛜 Your Kindle has a **Wi-Fi** connection. The more bars that appear, the stronger your connection.

3G 📶 Your Kindle is using a **3G** cellular network. (Only the Kindle 3G model has this indicator. At times the indicator represents an EDGE or GPRS network.)

✈ Your Paperwhite is in **Airplane** mode and has no wireless connection.

🔋 **Battery Status.** The battery indicator shows how much power remains. While your Kindle is charging, a lightning bolt appears within the battery indicator.

⚙ **Activity indicator:** This wheel icon appears in the top left corner of your screen while the Kindle is scanning or connecting to a network, downloading new content, checking for new items, or opening a large file or web page.

🔒 **Parental Controls indicator.** This indicates you've turned on specific restrictions or a Kindle FreeTime profile is active.

Setting Up Wi-Fi

A wireless network provides fast downloads of your Kindle books and other content. To view the available Wi-Fi networks:

1. From the **Home** screen, tap the **Menu** ≡ icon, then tap **Settings**.

2. Select the name of the Wi-Fi network you want to use. If a lock icon appears next to the network name, it requires a password.

Once you've connected to a network, the Wi-Fi status indicator at the top of the screen indicates the signal strength.

At left: The Paperwhite shows all
Wi-Fi networks within range of your
device.

Your Paperwhite will automatically find and connect with networks you've joined previously. The wireless indicator is located near the top-right corner of your screen, next to the battery indicator. A display of three bars indicates that your device is connected to a network with a strong signal. A series of dashes indicates your device isn't connected.

Trouble Connecting to a Wi-Fi Network

If you're unable to connect to a home network you've used previously, follow this procedure:

1. Turn off your Wi-Fi router and modem. Wait 30 seconds.

2. Press and hold your Paperwhite's **Power** button, then tap **Restart**.

3. Turn on your modem and wait while it restarts.

4. Turn on your router; wait for it to restart.

5. After your devices restart, try connecting to your Wi-Fi network again.

6.

Turning on Airplane Mode

You can turn off your 3G or Wi-Fi connection to conserve battery power or to use your Paperwhite while traveling on aircraft.

1. From **Home**, tap the **Menu** ☰ icon, then tap **Settings**.

2. Next to **Airplane** mode, tap **Off**. The switch will move to the **On** position. Now Airplane mode is on, and your wireless connection is off.

Connecting to a Mobile Network

If you purchased the 3G Paperwhite, it provides free 3G wireless service with no monthly fees or annual contracts.

Your Paperwhite automatically switches to Wi-Fi when available, which provides greater download speeds. If you're out of range of Wi-Fi, your device switches to a mobile connection when enabled.

Getting Help From Amazon

If you need to contact Amazon's customer support staff, click the "Contact Us" button on the right side of any help web page, such as www.Amazon.com/help and then choose your preferred method of contact, such as "phone," "email" or "chat." Using the contact form automatically informs Amazon's staff who you are, and it saves you the trouble of having to confirm your identify.

If you'd rather phone Amazon direct, the numbers are:

U.S. and Canada: 1-866-216-1072
Spanish Support: 866-749-7538
International: 1-206-266-2992

2 ► READING A BOOK, PAPERWHITE STYLE

After you've established a wireless connection, you're ready to go shopping. When you purchase a book, magazine or newspaper, it automatically downloads to your Paperwhite. Meanwhile, the content is also stored in the Cloud—so it's available to download to other Kindle devices or reading apps registered to your account.

Manage Your Payment Settings

All of your transactions with Amazon via the Paperwhite require a valid payment setting, even if you are downloading a free item. To view or change your payment setting:

1. Visit Manage Your Kindle (www.amazon.com/myk) and click **Kindle Payment Settings**.

2. Click **Edit**. This will launch the **Your Default 1-Click** payment setting page, where you can edit the settings.

3. Select your credit card information and click **Continue**. If desired, you can add a new card.

4. Enter your billing address and click **Continue**. You'll arrive at the **Kindle Payment Settings** page, where you can view your edited 1-Click payment method.

Shopping at the Kindle store

To visit the Kindle store, tap the **Shop** 🛒 icon.

When you're ready to purchase an item, tap the **Buy** button. (Or tap **Try Sample** to download and read the beginning of the item for free. To subscribe to a periodical, tap **Subscribe Now**.)

Tap the **Home** 🏠 icon to open your new content.

At left: Here's a book listing in Amazon's Kindle store. From here, you can buy the book, try a sample, or add it to your wish list.

Accidentally Purchasing a Book

If you buy a book by mistake, you can ask Amazon for a refund within seven days of purchase.

1. Visit **Manage Your Kindle** at www.amazon.com/myk

2. Beside the title, click **Actions**, then click **Return for refund**.

Undelivered Content

If you don't receive a book, app, video or other content after purchasing it, manually sync your device to check for pending downloads from the Amazon Cloud:

- From Home, tap the **Menu** ☰ icon, then tap **Sync & Check** for items. Titles pending delivery to your Kindle should begin downloading.

- If you still don't receive purchased content, check to ensure you have a wireless connection. Also, double-check to ensure your 1-Click payment method is still valid:

  1. Visit **Manage Your Kindle** at www.amazon.com/myk

  2. Under **Your Kindle Account**, click **Kindle Payment Settings**.

  3. Under **Your Default 1-Click Payment Method**, click **Edit** to review or edit your 1-Click payment settings.

View Your Reading Progress

With a paper-bound book, you have a simple reference point to judge your progress. By looking at the stack of pages, it's easy to see if you're halfway through a book, three-quarters of the way through, or somewhere in between. With Kindle books, you have three reference points—the number of "pages" read, the percentage of a book read, or the amount of time left in the chapter or book.

Location numbers – These are the digital equivalent of physical page numbers, and provide a way to easily reference a place in your reading material regardless of font size. The location displayed in a Kindle book is specific to the Kindle format and doesn't match the page number of printed editions.

Page numbers – These correspond to a book's printed edition. Not all Kindle books include page numbers. Because the font size and other elements are variable, it's possible to view more than one page (or less than a full page) on your screen at one time.

Time to Read – This feature uses your reading speed to calculate how much time is left before you finish your chapter or book.

While reading, tap the lower left corner of the screen to toggle between:

- Time left in chapter
- Time left in book
- Location numbers
- Page numbers (if available)

Another way to access your Reading Progress:

1. While reading, tap the top of the screen to show the reading toolbar.

2. Tap the **Menu** ≡ icon, then tap **Reading Progress**.

Select the tracking option you want displayed at the bottom of your screen:

- **Location in book**
- **Page in book** (if available)
- **Time left in chapter**
- **Time left in book**
- **None**

Jump to Other Locations in a Book

While reading, you can use **Page Flip** to skim other pages or sections and quickly jump back and forth without losing your place.

1. Tap the top of the screen to show the reading toolbar, then tap the bottom of the screen to launch a preview window and progress bar.

2. To view other locations in the book through the preview window:

    *   Swipe within the window, or tap the left or right arrows in the window.

    *   Press and drag the circle left or right in the progress bar at the bottom.

    *   Tap the left or right arrows at the bottom.

3. In the preview window, tap the page to go to that location in the book, or tap **X** in the top-right corner to return to your current place in the book.

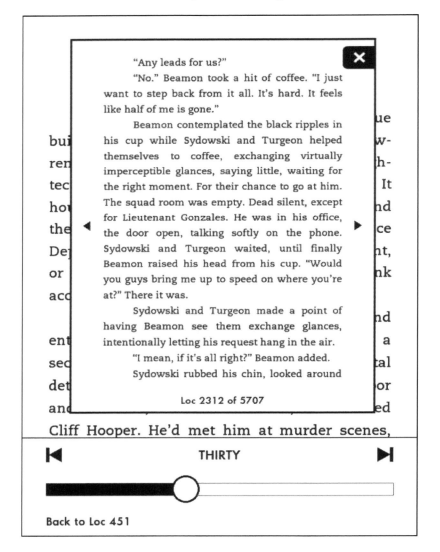

At left: Use the progress bar and preview window to glance at another location in a book.

Change Fonts, Line Spacing or Margins

You can change the fonts, font size, line spacing, or margins displayed for a Kindle book.

1. While reading, tap the top of your screen to display the reading toolbar, then tap **Aa**.

2. Change the text display for your book:

   - Font size – Select the size of the text.

   - Font type – Select the typeface of the text.

3. Set the line spacing and margins:

   - Line spacing – Select the amount of blank space to appear above and below each line.

   - Margins – Select the amount of space to appear on the left and right edges of each page.

4. Tap the **X** in the top-right corner to return to reading.

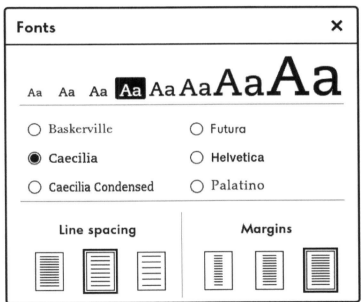

At left: From the reading toolbar, tap Aa to display options for changing fonts, line spacing or margins.

The text size of menus and other screens is fixed; you can't modify them. Likewise, you can't change the text appearance of PDF documents.

Manage Your Library

After you've accumulated dozens—or perhaps hundreds—of digital items, keeping track of it all might seem daunting. Fortunately, Amazon has a system that makes it simple. By visiting the **Manage Your Kindle** web page at www.amazon.com/myk, you can locate and deliver items from your Kindle Library to your Kindle devices or reading apps.

Deliver Items to Your Kindle

1. Visit **Manage Your Kindle** at www.amazon.com/myk

2. Under **Your Kindle Library**, locate the item you want to deliver.

3. Click **Actions**, then **Deliver to my** ...

4. Select your Paperwhite or reading app from the drop-down menu at **Deliver to my**...

5. Click **Deliver**. Your book or other content will be sent to your Paperwhite or reading app.

6. From your Kindle Paperwhite, go to the **Home** screen, and then tap the **On Device** tab to view and open the title.

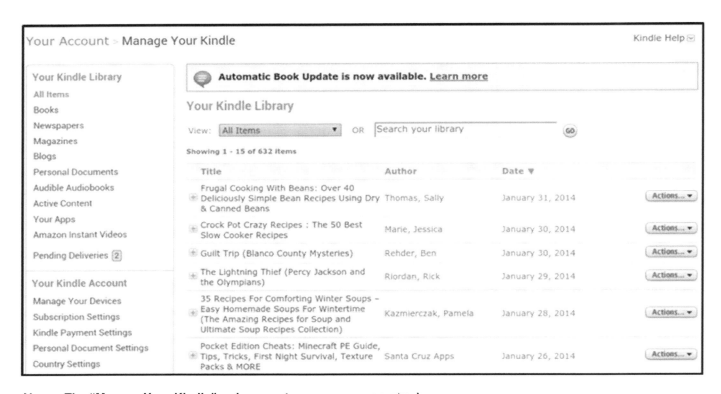

Above: The "Manage Your Kindle" web page at www.amazon.com/myk

Sync Your Paperwhite

Amazon's **Whispersync** feature enables you to synchronize all your Kindle content to all your devices and Kindle apps, including your books, audiobooks, personal documents, games, and Amazon Instant Video. For example, if you stop reading a book on your Paperwhite at the end of chapter one, the book will automatically open at the same point on all of your other Kindle devices and apps. Whispersync also makes your annotations available to all your devices, including bookmarks, highlights and notes.

Whispersync is enabled by default. To change the setting:

1. Visit **Manage Your Kindle** at www.amazon.com/myk

2. Under **Your Kindle Account**, click **Manage Your Devices**.

3. Under **Device Synchronization** (Whispersync Settings), tap the button for **Whispersync Device Synchronization** (on or off).

Occasionally you'll want to "sync" your Paperwhite, which can serve two functions for you: First, you'll prompt your Paperwhite to check for and download any awaiting items. Secondly, it syncs items you might be reading on other Kindle devices or apps—so you can automatically resume reading at the place you left off, even if you switch devices.

- From Home, tap the **Menu** ☰ icon, then tap **Sync & Check for Items**. Titles that were delivered to your Kindle—and saved bookmarks and annotations—should begin downloading to your Paperwhite.

- While reading, tap the **Menu** ☰ icon, then tap **Sync to the Furthest Page Read**. When you're finished reading, make it a habit to return to the **Home** screen, which records your reading progress and prevents syncing errors.

Use Bookmarks, Highlights and Notes

You can add, view or remove bookmarks within Kindle books or personal documents.

- Add a bookmark:

  1. Tap the top-right corner of the screen to show the **Bookmark** ⌐ icon, then tap + and the Bookmark icon will turn black ▮.

- View your bookmarks:

  1. Tap the top-right corner of the screen to show the Bookmark ⌐ icon. A list of your bookmarks appears.

- Tap a bookmark in the list to preview that location in the book. Tap the preview window to jump to that location in the book.

- Remove a bookmark:

  1. Tap the top-right corner of the screen to show the **Bookmark** ⬜ icon.

  2. Tap a bookmark in the list, then tap **X** to delete that bookmark.

Add, View or Remote Highlights

You can add, view or remove highlights within a Kindle book or personal document.

- **Highlight a word:** Press and hold the word, tap **More**, then tap **Highlight**.

- **Highlight a phrase:** Press and drag to highlight the desired passage, then tap **Highlight**.

- **Highlight multiple pages:** Press and drag to highlight the desired text to the bottom-right corner of the page. The page will turn and the highlight will automatically continue to the first period on the next page. You can drag the handle at the start or end of the highlighted text to refine your selection.

- **Remove a highlight:** Press and hold a word in the highlighted area, tap **More**, and then tap **Delete**.

- **View your highlights:**

  1. Tap the top of the screen to display the reading toolbar, tap **Go To**, then tap the **Notes** tab.

  2. Tap the **Yours** tab to view notes and highlights you've created. Tap a note or highlight to jump to that location in the book.

Add, View, Edit or Remove Notes

You can add, view, edit or remove notes within a Kindle book or personal document.

- Add a note:

  1. Press and hold a word or press and drag to highlight the desired text. If you selected a word, tap **More**, tap **Add Note**, and then type your desired text. If you selected a phrase, tap **Add Note**, then type your text.

  2. Tap **Save** to create your note.

- Edit a note:

  1. Tap the number where the note appears, then tap **Edit Note**.

  2. Make your chnages, then tap **Save**.

- Remove a Note:

1. Tap the number where the note appears, then tap **More**.

2. Tap **Delete Note**.

- View your notes:

    1. Tap the top of the screen to display the reading toolbar, tap the **Menu** ☰ icon, then then tap **Notes**.

    2. Tap **Yours** to view notes and highlights you've created. Tap a note or highlight to jump to that location in the book.

View Popular Highlights and Public Notes

Amazon displays Popular Highlights and Public Notes by combining input from all Kindle users and identifying the passages with the most highlights and notes.

- To turn on Popular Highlights or Public Notes:

    1. While reading, tap the top of the screen to show the reading toolbar.

    2. Tap the **Menu** ☰ icon and then tap **Settings**.

    3. Tap **Reading Options** and then tap **Notes & Highlights**.

    4. Beside **Popular Highlights** or **Public Notes**, tap **Off**. The switch moves to the **On** position. When you resume reading, frequently selected highlights will appear as you read.

- To view a list of Popular Highlights or Public Notes:

    1. While reading, tap the top of your screen to display the reading toolbar.

    2. Tap **Go To**, then tap the **Notes** tab.

Book Lovers, Rejoice: Free Books!

Kindle Buffet is a daily website that features a hand-picked list of great Kindle books being offered free that day. Includes mysteries, romance, science-fiction, horror, non-fiction and more. Today's bestsellers and yesterday's classics. You may never need to pay for a book again! See for yourself by visiting www.KindleBuffet.com

Free books, all you can eat!

Allison (A Kane Novel)

Mystery, Thriller & Suspense
Author: Steve Gannon

Allison Kane, a journalism student at UCLA, takes a summer job as a TV news intern—soon becoming involved in a scandalous murder investigation and the media firestorm that follows—a position that pits her squarely against her iron-fisted police detective father.

Cafenova (Clairmont Series)

Christian Fiction > Romance
Author: S. Jane Scheyder

Leaving her broken heart behind in Seattle, Maddy Jacobs starts a new life on the coast of Maine. Although running a Bed and Breakfast has always been her dream, restoring the sprawling Victorian inn is a massive undertaking. Her contractor, competent, handsome, and built like a Greek god, could be the answer to her prayers. If she can keep her wits about her, she might just survive the summer.

20 Things I've Learned as an Entrepreneur

Small Business & Entrepreneurship
Author: Alicia Morga

20 Things I've Learned as an Entrepreneur is the summary of lessons leading female technology entrepreneur Alicia Morga learned as a first-time entrepreneur in Silicon Valley. If you're an entrepreneur or if you've only dreamed about starting your own business, this quick important read is for you.

3 ► FEED YOUR KINDLE WITH FREE CONTENT

Finding free content for your Paperwhite isn't difficult. In fact, you'll find that there are plenty of sites out there—including Amazon itself—offering free content of one type or another. These sites may offer a variety of different types of content, from video to audio to books. While you're exploring them, you'll want to avoid illegal pirate sites.

Now, for the good news: There is actually a ton of free content out there that you can download for your Paperwhite and, better yet, it's entirely legal.

Public Domain Books

Many older popular books are no longer under copyright, and so they're in the "Public Domain" and usually available free in e-book formats. For instance, the works of Edgar Allen Poe, Mary Shelly, Jane Austin and Charlotte Bronte were written so long ago, nobody owns the rights anymore. There is a caveat here, however.

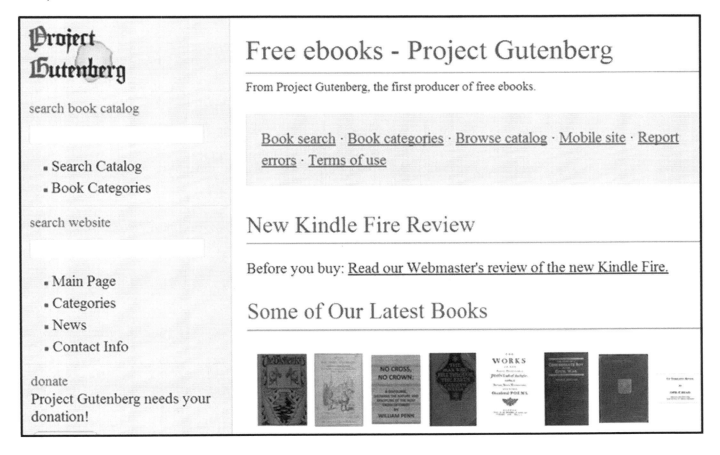

If you buy a specific publisher's edition of a public domain work, that edition is copyrighted. The edition likely has unique material in it that does fall under the copyright protection of the publisher and, therefore, it cannot be reproduced in full. To put it in shorthand terms: You can reproduce *The Raven* all you want, but you cannot reproduce a copyrighted analysis of *The Raven* included in a printing of the poem.

There are several sites that offer public domain books. The most well-known is likely Project Gutenberg, located at www.gutenberg.org

Exploring Project Gutenberg

The illustration above shows the Project Gutenberg homepage. The left navigation menu gives you access to the site's entire book catalog. You can choose to **Search Catalog**, **Browse Catalog** or you can view **Book Categories**.

Let's search for a well-known suspense story, *The Turn of the Screw* by Henry James. Here is the result from Project Gutenberg:

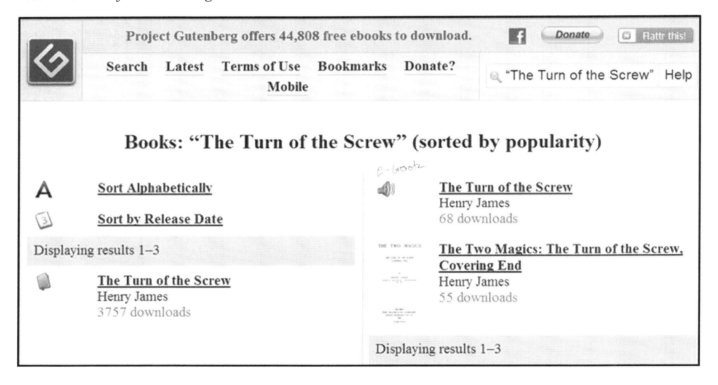

Above: Search results for *Turn of the Screw* at Project Gutenberg.

Notice that, on the right of the page, there are two results listed. The first result is a link to the e-book version. The second result is a link to the audio version of the story. (Project Gutenberg has a lot of audio books that are public domain and that are read by volunteers. If you want to stock up on audio books for a long trip, this is a good place to do it!)

Let's click on the link to the e-book version of *The Turn of the Screw*.

Above: The e-book versions of *The Turn of the Screw*

Project Gutenberg will typically offer books in a variety of formats. Notice that there are HTML, EPUB, Kindle, PLocker, QiOO Mobile and Plain Text versions of this e-book.

Simply click on the link to download the e-book and save it to your computer. You can either transfer the book to your Paperwhite manually or you can do so through your Calibre library, which will allow you to assign it a cover and other metadata, as I did with *The Raven*.

Public Domain Books on Amazon

Like Project Gutenberg, Amazon offers thousands of classic Public Domain works absolutely free. These books remain free all year long, and many of them are the same texts available through Project Gutenberg.

Let's do a search for "Bronte" on Amazon.com. This will bring up books by the Bronte sisters. On the right side of the web page, select **Price—Low to High** and the free public domain books will appear.

TIP: Many rare and out-of-print books are now available as e-books from several different sites. If you've been searching for a book that means a lot to you to own—maybe something from your childhood or with similar sentimental value—be sure to check Project Gutenberg and Amazon. It may well be available on one of these sites.

Even though a particular book might be "free," you'll still need a 1-Click payment method at Amazon to download them. You'll get a receipt in your email that will show the purchase but nothing will show up on your credit card or bank statement.

Lend or Borrow Kindle Books

Remember the days when you'd loan your paperback books to friends, and (depending on the friend) rarely see the book again? Well, a great feature of lending books via your Kindle is that all your books will actually be returned—there's no way around it. Loans are capped at 14 days by Amazon's system.

Not all Kindle books are eligible for lending—the publisher has to agree to the program. When you're shopping for Kindle books nowadays, you'll see a notation—whether lending is **enabled** or not—in the **Product Details** of the book's listing on Amazon.

TIP: Remember, you can loan Kindle books to virtually anyone with an email address, regardless of whether they have a Kindle device. They can read the book on a free Kindle reading app on their computer or smartphone. Kindle reading apps are available free for practically every type of computer, smartphone, and other digital gadgets.

You're allowed to lend Kindle books only once per title. During the loan period, you won't have access to the book.

Visit the Kindle store and locate the product page for the book.

From the product page, click **Loan this book**.

Enter the borrower's email address (their regular email address, not a Kindle address) and an optional personal message.

Click **Send Now**.

You can also loan Kindle books from the **Manage Your Kindle** page at www.amazon.com/myk . In the **Actions** menu, select **Loan this title**. Borrowers can return loaned books via **Manage Your Kindle**.

Borrow Books From the Kindle Owner's Lending Library

Amazon Prime members can borrow one book per month from the Kindle Owner's Lending Library with no due dates. Not all books are eligible for borrowing.

1. Tap the top of the screen to reveal the toolbar, then tap the **Kindle Store** icon.

2. Near the top-right corner of the screen, tap **All Categories**.

3. Tap **Kindle Owners' Lending Library**.

Eligible titles display the Prime badge: **✔Prime**

Amazon Prime charges an annual fee and offers many benefits. If you're not a member and like the idea of the Lending Library, you may want to look into Prime's offerings, which include free videos and free two-day shipping on eligible products. See http://bit.ly/amazonPrime

Borrow Books From a Public Library

You can borrow Kindle books from the websites of local libraries and have them sent to your Kindle or reading app. About 11,000 U.S. libraries offer Kindle books. Just like regular library books, Kindle books may be loaned for a specific period of time. Since only one copy of a Kindle book may be loaned at one time, there might be a waiting period before you can borrow a popular title.

Confirm whether your library branch carries Kindle books. Visit your library's website or visit Overdrive, the company that handles library Kindle lending at www.search.overdrive.com

Obtain a library card and PIN from your local library.

Search for Kindle books at your library's website.

At checkout, sign into your Amazon account, and select your Kindle device.

Your Kindle should receive the book automatically. If not, sync your device manually.

Amazon sends a courtesy email to remind you three days before the book is due, and another message after the loan period ends. To return the book before the loan period ends, visit **Manage Your Kindle** at www.amazon.com/myk . Click **Actions**, then **Return This Book**.

A Whole New Calibre of Reading Material

Amazon benefits mightily from consumer loyalty. By linking their device so strongly to the AZW and MOBI formats they use, they make the average user assume they can only read e-books that are bought directly from Amazon. Fortunately, you actually can read any e-book format you want, thanks to a great program called Calibre, a program that runs on Windows or Mac desktop computers. Calibre can find all sorts of valuable non-Amazon content and format it and deliver it to your Kindle.

Calibre is free, it's stable and, to put it in the most direct terms, it's awesome—it can deliver you hundreds of dollars' worth of newspaper, magazine and book content every day, 365 days a year. The only challenge is finding the time to read that gusher of great content you're piping to your Paperwhite.

Let's jump right in and download the Calibre application to your computer. I have been using the program, along with thousands of others, for the past three years. The best things in life are free, and believe me, Calibre is one of them.

1. Go to www.calibre-ebook.com and select **Download Calibre**.

2. Open the downloaded program to install the package once it's completed.

3. On your first run, you'll get the **Welcome Wizard**. This is designed to help you set up your libraries and to import your books, as well as to help you select the correct device!

4. The first screen will set your Calibre Library directory. The default choice is a good one. On the next screen, you'll have to choose your device. Choose your Paperwhite, of course.

This sets the program up so that it knows to look for your Kindle when you click the Send to Device icon.

When you have the program installed, launch it, and study the interface for a moment. This program is capable of doing many things; even offering you a way to shop for content across a number of different stores. What we'll concern ourselves with first, however, is opening up new sources of literature by using the features built into this program that allow you to convert books from other formats into ones that your Amazon Kindle can read.

All the News You Can Eat, and Calibre Picks Up the Check

Okay, I'll admit it. I'm a book nut. But I have an even bigger problem. I'm addicted to newspapers, too. I was a "news junkie" before anyone ever heard of such a thing. Twenty-five years ago, I paid about $75 a month to have three different newspapers dropped at my doorstep every morning—my local paper, the *Wall Street Journal*, and the *New York Times*.

Now, since I discovered Calibre, I've been reading six newspapers a day—plus bunch of blogs and magazines like *Newsweek* and *Time*—and it doesn't cost me one red cent. The *Washington Post*. The *New York Post*. And, if I still have time, I can read the *Onion* and a couple others—just to get my humor fix. Your local newspaper is probably available, too. Calibre downloads the content they post on their websites, and sends it, nicely formatted, to your Kindle. The only cost is the few minutes you'll spend setting it up once, and then it works every day. Here how to get started:

1. Click on **Fetch News** in the menu.

2. Select your language.

3. Select a news source.

4. In the next illustration, you can see that I've selected the *Washington Post*.

Note that I've opted to have it download automatically every day of the week after 6am. If you were the ultimate news junkie, you could set it to download the Associated Press news wire every 10 minutes.

Calibre has hundreds of different news sources available in a huge number of languages, you just click them and enjoy—free.

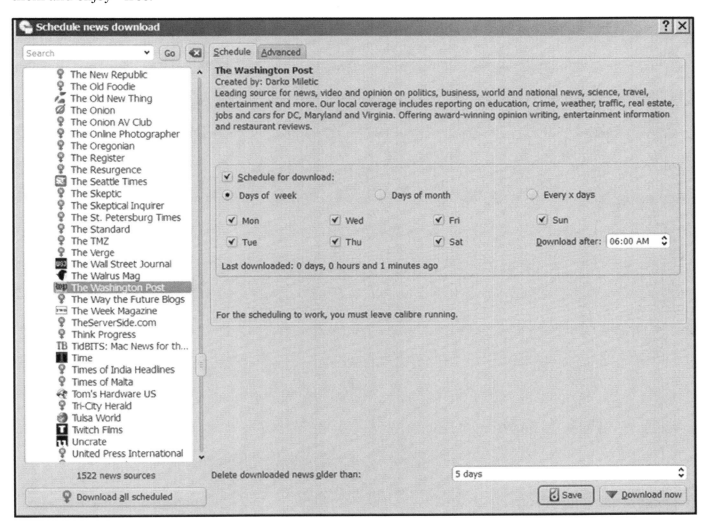

Above: Selecting the *Washington Post* news download.

Of course, you have to leave Calibre running so it automatically downloads your news sources. If you have several news sites on your list, it will take a while. Personally, I leave my computer on 24/7, and Calibre is finding news for me constantly, and feeding my Kindle. In the old days, I used to finish my three newspapers and still want more. Now, with Calibre, I don't have a prayer of skimming everything I'm tempted to read every day.

TIP: In this section, we're talking about downloading content for free. It sounds too good to be true, but it's totally above board. We're not stealing, we're just using the stuff that publishers are posting to their websites. Calibre simply does the work of formatting it for the Kindle and emailing it to us.

After the news site has converted, you'll be able to transfer it to your Kindle using the same interface that you use to transfer books. One of the best things about the Calibre program is that it's smart in meaningful ways. The program, for instance, will transfer newspapers to your Newsstand.

E-Books, Calibre and the Kindle

Believe it or not, there's more to the story. In addition to newspapers and magazines, you can manage e-books—downloaded from Amazon and elsewhere—using Calibre.

Above: Calibre's main screen

In the illustration above, I haven't added my e-books to the collection yet, so the middle of the screen is blank. There are many ways you can add books to your library. By default, they're sent to the **Calibre Library** folder.

The **Add Books** icon appears at the upper left. Select it, and you'll see the options shown below.

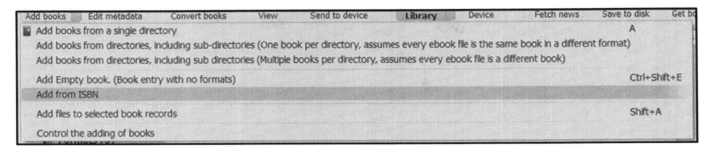

Above: The Add Books dialog

There are quite a few options here, but we'll concentrate adding one book to the library in a format that Kindle just doesn't like.

In this case, I'm going to add a book that's stored in the EPUB format—a popular one on many sites—that I want to read on my Paperwhite in the native Kindle AZW or MOBI format.

To start, click on **Add books from a single directory** and browse to the directory that you want. In the illustration below, I've chosen the book "pg1062.epub" which is actually *The Raven* by Edgar Allen Poe, which I have in the EPUB format that the Kindle will not read. I downloaded it from Project Gutenberg, a site that has plenty of public domain eBooks to choose from.

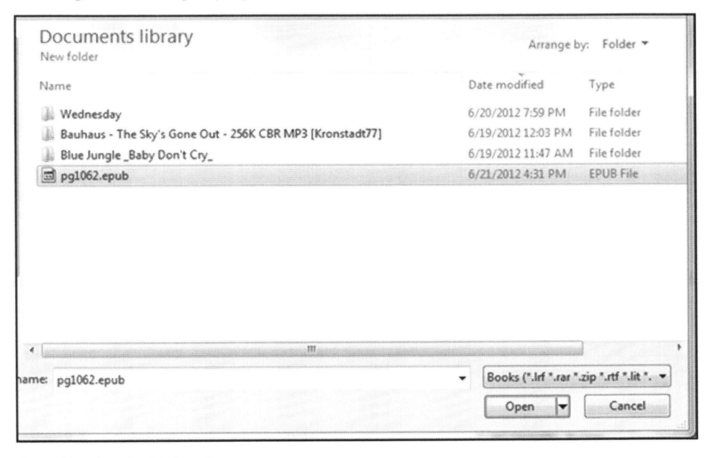

Above: Choosing a book to import

In the illustration below, you can see that the book has been added to my **Calibre Library**. Notice that even the cover art came over with the import, as did the description and other metatag information. This is one of the handiest features with the Calibre program. I'll change it to more suitable cover art and change the metatags during the conversion process so that they're more descriptive and accurate.

Above: The e-book from Project Gutenberg now appears in My Library.

Before I move this to my Paperwhite, I have to convert it. Fortunately, Calibre makes that very easy to do.

Highlight the title and select the **Convert Books** icon and then select **Convert individually**. The screen pictured below appears.Take a look at the options available. The **Metadata** selection controls the description, publisher credit, and other information associated with the book. Be sure to fill these out if they're not filled out already. They're important organizational tools.

Above: The Convert screen

You can also change the cover image, which I've done using a public domain cover that I downloaded. I could technically use any image I wanted, however, as long as it doesn't violate anyone's copyright. You can change the **Look and Feel** of the output, which alters the text formatting, and more. One thing that Calibre does very well is give you options!

Because this book needs to be readable on the Paperwhite, we'll go with the MOBI format, which you can see in the upper right-most dropdown list.

TIP: You can convert more than one file at once, but it takes a lot of time. If you're going to do so, you might want to get a cup of coffee, order a pizza, or do something else to pass the time. If you have a slow computer, consider making your own pizza from scratch!

Now, the file has been converted to the MOBI format, which the Paperwhite will be entirely happy with, but we have to move it over to the Paperwhite, of course.

Select, **Send to Device** from the top menu on the main screen. It will pick the device that you set up during the **Welcome Wizard**. Because the Paperwhite doesn't take an SD card, you can just choose

Send to Main Memory from the dropdown list. If you did have a device with additional onboard storage, Calibre would give you the option to send it to that storage.

Above: Sending the book to the Kindle.

When the book has been sent, you'll see the listing for it under the **On Device** heading change. If I go to my **Books Library** on my Paperwhite and look under the titles available on my device, it shows right up.

This is only one of the functions that Calibre offers you. It's an amazingly powerful program. We'll explore it more, but be aware that this is going to be one of your most important resources for getting free books off of the Internet. The sites that offer works from the public domain sometime don't have them in a format that the Kindle reads. In the future, of course, a format may come along that is incompatible with your Kindle books. Instead of having to buy them in a new format, you'll just be able to convert them!

Let's Go Shopping!

The Paperwhite makes it easy to go shopping at Amazon, and Calibre makes it easy to go shopping everywhere else. Because it can convert e-books to different formats, that means that you can hit Amazon, Barnes & Noble, Borders, Project Gutenberg or any other site out there and purchase and download books without worrying about the format.

Click on the **Get Books** icon on the top of the screen. Because I also have Cherie Priest's book *Boneshaker* on my Calibre and Kindle, I'll get the option to **Search This Author**, which I'll do.

If I wanted to, however, I could search for any book using the **Search for E-books** option. I found *The Raven* using that search function. The following search dialog will come up. Along the left hand side of the dialog, pictured below, you'll see options for which stores to search.

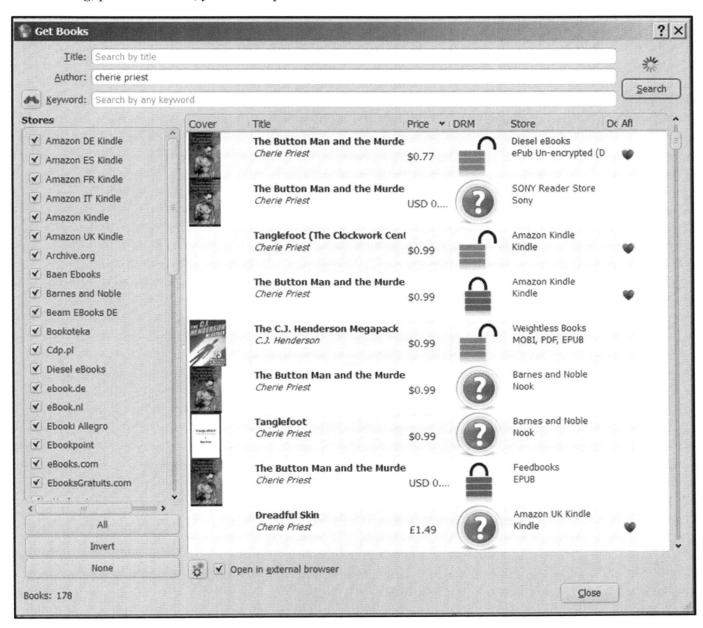

Above: Just part of the Search Results

Notice the locks that appear next to some of the listings. This indicates whether the book has DRM (Digital Rights Management, or copy prevention). This doesn't mean that you cannot move them from device to device, but you need an additional program to do it. It's called Adobe Digital Editions, which is also valuable for downloading books from your public library. Adobe Digital Editions allows you to authorize your e-reader, which allows the publisher to manage the DRM properly.

Clicking on any of the links in the search results will take you to the appropriate page where you can buy the book. This is an amazing feature, when you think about it. Amazon has just about everything in the way of books, of course, but there are always those books that they don't have and you can search other stores to find them if you need to.

The search feature also searches public domain sources for books. Sort the books by price or by DRM status to get to the public domain versions, if one is available.

Kindlefeeder

Another popular third-party Kindle service is Kindlefeeder.com. Like Calibre, it enables you to send content that appears on the Internet to your Kindle via email. I suppose it's a bit easier to use at first, but doesn't have the range of Calibre. See www.kindlefeeder.com

4 ▶ CREATE AND VIEW PERSONAL DOCUMENTS

One of the strongest features of the Paperwhite is its compact size. It's easy to tote around and, if you wish, it can often take the place of a laptop computer. If you're going to use your Kindle frequently as an e-reader or productivity tool, taking advantage of Amazon's **Personal Documents Service** is a must. Although Amazon's Kindle books use a proprietary format—you need a Kindle (or a Kindle app) to read them—you can send virtually any kind of digital document to your Kindle using the Personal Documents Service.

You can use the Personal Documents Service along with your **Send-to-Kindle** email address. The email address is usually formatted as follows: [Your Name]@Kindle.com

If you're unsure of your Send-to-Kindle address, you can review it at Amazon's **Manage Your Kindle** web page at www.amazon.com/myk

Kindle Personal Documents Service

You can send documents to your Kindle using either the **Send to Kindle** application or from an email address you've authorized (this procedure is explained in the following section). Attach the document to an email and send it to your **Send-to-Kindle email address**, which is a unique email address automatically assigned by Amazon.

Documents that you send to your Send-to-Kindle email address are stored in the Cloud and synced across all compatible Kindle devices and reading apps. The documents appear in the **Docs** library on your Kindle.

To change your Send-to-Kindle email address, visit **Manage Your Kindle** at www.amazon.com/myk and click **Personal Documents Settings**.

Under **Send-to-Kindle email address**, click **Edit**.

Enter the new address, and click **Update**.

If your document needs to be converted to Kindle's .azw format, enter "convert" in the email's subject line.

Your Approved Personal Document Email List

Your Kindle can only receive documents from email addresses you've approved. The regular email address registered with your Amazon account is already added to the approved list.

To edit your **Approved Personal Document Email** list:

1. Visit **Manage Your Kindle** at www.amazon.com/myk and click **Personal Document Settings**.

2. Under **Approved Personal Document Email** list, select **Add** a new approved email address.

3. Enter the new email address and click **Add Address**.

Converting Documents

One of the best features of the Personal Documents Service is that it can automatically convert most common document formats to the Kindle format, called AZW. You don't have to know the technical details, it just works. Then once the document is on your Kindle, you can use many of the functions available with Kindle documents—you can make annotations, change the font, adjust the text size, and so forth. To convert your documents, enter the word Convert in the subject line of the email.

TIP: Don't use Personal Documents Service for commercial purposes, such as sending out a commercial newsletter. It's against Amazon's terms of service, and that's why it's called the Personal Documents Service.

Transfer Personal Documents via USB Cable

Let's say you want to transfer a document from your computer to your Kindle via USB cable, and you need to convert the document to Kindle's .azw format. Before you can accomplish this, you'll need to change your Send-to-Kindle email address to the name [your-name]@free.kindle.com and then enter "convert" in the subject line of your email.

To download the converted document to your computer, follow the instructions Amazon puts in the email.

Choose your desktop, then click **Save**.

Connect your Kindle to your computer with the USB cable. (On a Windows computer, navigate to the Kindle by browsing My Computer. (On Macs, the Kindle will appear on your desktop.)

Click on the Kindle to browse the Kindle's drive.

Drag your document from your desktop and drop it into the **Documents** folder of the Kindle drive.

Eject your Kindle device and unplug the USB cable.

Supported File Types for Kindle Personal Documents Service

The following file types can be automatically converted to the Kindle format .azw by sending them in an email with "convert" in the subject line:

Microsoft Word (.doc, .docx)

HTML (.html, .htm)

RTF (.rtf)

Text (.txt)

JPEG (.jpeg, .jpg)

Kindle Format (.mobi, .azw)

GIF (.gif)

PNG (.png)

BMP (.bmp)

PDF (.pdf)

'Send to Kindle' Application

Another way to send documents to your Kindle is by using the **Send to Kindle** application, a free program you can install on your computer. With it, you can send content such as word-processing documents, news articles, blog posts and other content to your Kindle.

The Send-to-Kindle application is quite efficient and easy to use, and it automatically converts documents to the Kindle format.

Download the program by visiting www.amazon.com/gp/sendtokindle and following the instructions. After entering your Amazon email address and password, click **Register**. If you own more than one Kindle device, you can select which device(s) will receive the documents.

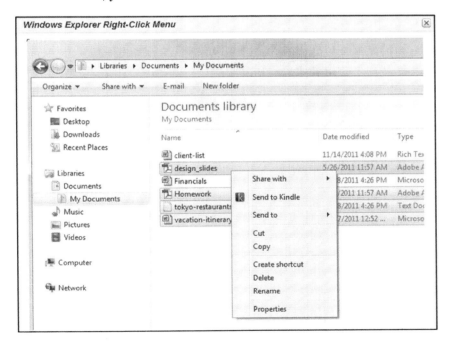

At left: Using the right-click function of the Send-to-Kindle for PC application

Send-to-Kindle is also available as a browser extension for the Chrome and Firefox Web browsers.

Download From the Cloud

All of your Kindle content is saved to the Cloud and available for download to your Paperwhite. Let's imagine that you want to download a previously purchased Kindle book to your Paperwhite.

From the **Home** screen, tap **Books** to open its content library.

Tap **Cloud** (instead of **Device**) to display the books you own that haven't been downloaded to your Kindle.

Tap the **book** image to download it to your device. Items that have been downloaded to your Paperwhite have a check mark in the lower right corner of the cover image. Items stored in the Cloud do not have a check mark.

5 ▶ ADVANCED TIPS AND TRICKS

Once you've accumulated a few dozen books and other documents, it becomes hard to find what you're looking for. Perhaps you need a special place where you can pigeon-hole the 27 Thanksgiving cookbooks scattered throughout your Paperwhite. Fortunately, there's a solution: organizing those items into custom categories stored in the Cloud. You can add as many items as you wish to these **Cloud Collections**, including books, personal documents, and active content. (Newspapers, magazines and blogs can't be added to collections.)

Organize your content with Cloud Collections

1. To create a new collection:

   - From **Home**, tap the **Menu** ≡ icon, then tap **Create New Collection**.

   - Enter a name for the collection, then tap **OK**. A list appears of items eligible to be added to the collection.

   - Tap the checkbox next to a title to add it to the collection.

   - Tap **Done** when finished. The new collection will show up on the **Home** screen.

2. To edit or delete a collection:

   - From **Home**, press and hold the collection title.

   - Tap to **Add/Remove Items**, **Rename This Collection**, or **Delete This Collection**.

Deleting a collection doesn't erase a book or other documents from your Kindle library. However, if you delete a collection, that collection is also deleted from the Cloud and your other Kindle devices and apps.

Viewing and Managing Your Cloud Collections

Once you've established a few Cloud Collections, you'll probably want to customize the way you view and access them on your Paperwhite. You can also **star** your favorites to make them even more accessible.

1. To filter your items on the Home screen:

   - From **Home**, tap **My Items**. You'll see options to view **All Items** or only **Books**, **Periodicals**, **Docs**, **Collections**, or **Active Content**.

   - Tap **Collections** to view all your collections.

2. To star a collection:

- Press and hold a collection cover, then tap **Show in All Views**. A star appears in the bottom-right corner of the collection cover. The collection will appear on your Home screen when you view **All Items** or **Collections**. The collection also appears when you view **Books**, **Docs**, or **Active Content** if it contains books, personal documents, or active content, respectively.

3. To unstar a collection:

- Press and hold a starred collection cover, then tap **Show Only in Collections View**. A star will no longer appear on the collection cover, and the collection will only appear on your Home screen when you view **Collections**.

Fixing a Slow or Frozen Screen

If your screen is slow to respond or freezes, try rebooting your device. Press and hold the power button for about five seconds. When the prompt appears on your screen, tap **Restart**. (Don't worry, restarting will not remove content or deregister your device.)

At left: Press and hold the power button to restart your Paperwhite.

On/Off button

If the trouble persists, check your battery level and the cleanliness of your screen. Keep in mind, your device may respond slowly while downloading large items. Also, check to see if your device is using the most recent software updates. For more information, see the address below:

www.amazon.com/gp/help/customer/display.html?nodeId=200529680

The last resort in fixing a frozen Paperwhite is resetting the device to the factory default settings.

1. From the **Home** screen, tap the **Menu** ☰ icon.

2. Tap **Settings**.

3. Tap **Menu** again, then tap **Reset Device**.

After resetting, you'll need to register your device again and download content from your Kindle library.

Deregister Your Paperwhite

If your Paperwhite is registered to the wrong Amazon account—or if you're no longer going to use it to buy content, you can deregister the device from your Amazon account. You can deregister while using your device, or while at Amazon's website.

After deregistering the device, you will no longer have access to your Kindle library or items previously downloaded through Kindle applications running on your smartphone or other devices.

After the deregistration process, you can Register the device to a different Amazon account.

From your device:

1. From the **Home** screen, tap the **Menu** ≡ icon, then tap **Settings**.

2. Tap **Registration**.

3. In the **Deregister Your Kindle** box, tap **Deregister**.

From your computer:

1. Visit Manage Your Kindle at www.amazon.com/myk and then click **Manage Your Devices**.

2. Click the image of your Paperwhite, then click **Deregister**.

Set up Parental Controls

If you have young children in the home, the Parental Controls settings will provide you with peace of mind while your child uses the Kindle. You can restrict access to shopping, the web browser, and disable the ability to deregister and reset your Paperwhite.

1. From **Home**, tap the Menu ≡ icon, then tap **Settings**.

2. Tap **Device Options**, then tap **Parental Controls**.

3. Tap **Off** to require a password to the web browser, Kindle store, or cloud.

4. Provide a Parental Controls password, then tap **OK**.

5. Tap OK to save your Parental Controls settings.

When Parental Controls are set, a **lock** 🔒 icon appears at the top of the screen.

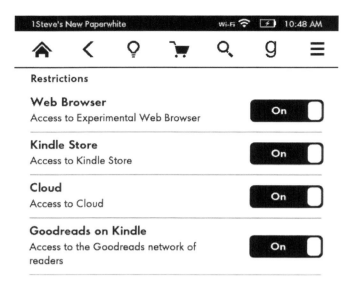

At left: With Parental Controls, you can prevent accidental access to the store and web browser.

When access to the Kindle Store is locked on your Paperwhite, you can continue purchasing and delivering content from your computer.

Transferring Content From a Computer to Your Paperwhite

In addition to Wi-Fi, you can also use a USB cord to transfer files from your computer to your Paperwhite. First, we'll download a document from your Kindle library to your computer:

1. Visit **Manage Your Kindle** at www.amazon.com/myk and locate the Kindle content you want to transfer.

2. From the **Actions** drop-down menu, click **Download & Transfer via USB**.

3. From the drop-down menu, select your Kindle, then click **Download**. You might be prompted to "open" or "save" the file. Select "save" and select an easy-to-remember location, such as your computer's desktop.

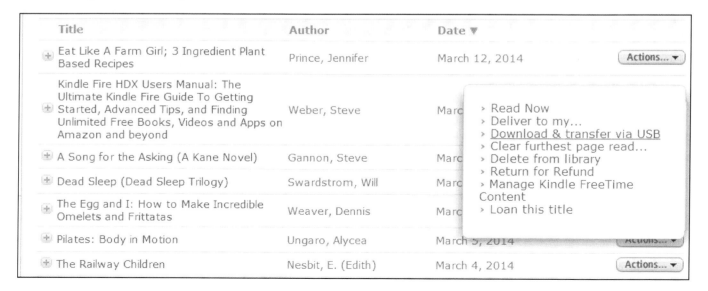

Above: Downloading a file from the "Manage Your Kindle" web page.

Now we'll transfer the document from your computer to your Kindle via USB:

1. Connect your Kindle to your computer using the USB cord. (On Windows computers, your Kindle will appear in the same location as external USB drives, usually the **My Computer** menu. On Macs, your Kindle will appear on the desktop.)

2. Locate the downloaded file on your computer, then drag and drop the file into the **Documents** folder in the Kindle folder.

3. Eject your Kindle from your computer by right-clicking your Kindle and selecting **Eject**.

4. On your Kindle, tap **Home** 🏠 and **On Device** to view your content.

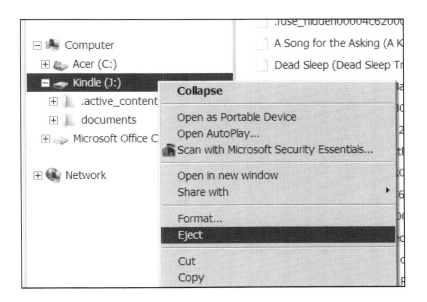

At left: Ejecting the
Paperwhite from a PC

Change Your Device Language

You can set your default language to English (U.S.), English (U.K.), German, French (France), French (Canada), Italian, Spanish (Spain), Spanish (Mexico), Portuguese (Brazil), Japanese, and Chinese (Simplified).

1. From **Home**, tap the **Menu** ≡ icon, then tap **Settings**.

2. Tap **Device Options**, then tap **Language and Dictionaries**, then tap one of these options:

   - **Language:** Pick a different language for your device.

   - **Keyboard:** Pick a region-specific layout for the keyboard.

   - **Dictionaries:** Set the default dictionary for each language.

When you pick a new language, the device menus, keyboard, and default dictionary are changed accordingly. If you purchase a book in a different language, the dictionary and keyboard for that language is downloaded to your Paperwhite automatically. The default dictionary and keyboard changes based on the language of the book you're reading.

Enjoy Enhanced Reading Features

Simply reading a book is just scratching the surface when it comes to the Paperwhite. You can learn more about the book, easily look up words in the dictionary, and translate text.

Exploring Books with X-Ray

X-Ray lets you explore the structure of a book. You can also dig for more background information from Wikipedia and Shelfari, Amazon's community for book lovers. X-Ray isn't available for all books—if it's not available, the X-Ray option is grayed out.

1. While reading, tap the top of the screen to display the reading toolbar, then tap **X-Ray**.

2. View and filter the list of topics:

    •   To filter by section of the book, tap **Page**, **Chapter** or **Book**.

    •   To filter by the type of topic, tap **People** or **Terms**.

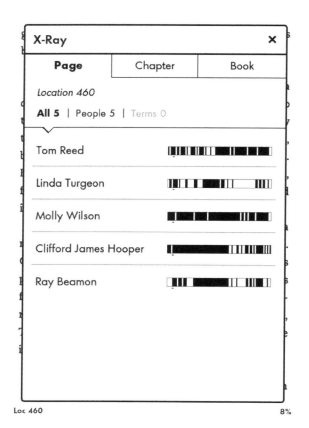

At left: With the X-Ray feature, the bars show all of the locations in the page, chapter or book where that character or term is mentioned.

3. To learn more about a topic or character, tap the item in the list. Then you can read a description, see links to Wikipedia or Shelfari, or excerpts in the book mentioning the term.

4. When you're finished, tap the Back ◀ button or the **X** to resume reading.

TIP: Here's a shortcut to these enhanced features: While reading, press and hold a word or character name to launch the **Smart Lookup** window, where you can view Dictionary, X-Ray or Wikipedia information. Smart Lookup classifies the type of term you're looking up, and adjust the tabs accordingly.

Use the Dictionary

One of the most powerful features of the Kindle is the ease of accessing dictionary definitions. Instead of interrupting your reading to grab a dictionary from your bookshelf, you can access instant information from the Paperwhite's built-in dictionary.

1. While reading, press and hold a word, then release to launch the **Smart Lookup** window.

2. Scroll within the **Dictionary** tab to view the full definition.

3. Tap outside the window to resume reading.

Expand Your Vocabulary

When you look up words in your Paperwhite's dictionary, they're automatically added to the **Vocabulary Builder** on the device. This feature generates flashcards, which you can use to test your retention of word definitions and usages.

1. From **Home**, tap the **Menu** ☰ icon, then tap **Vocabulary Builder**. You'll see a list of all words you've looked up with the dictionary. There are separate tabs for **Books** (words you looked up within a specific book), **Learning** (words available as flashcards) and **Mastered** (words you marked as "mastered" and no longer included in flashcards).

2. Tap **Flashcards** at the bottom of the screen to begin testing yourself of the list of words.

3. To turn off **Vocabulary Builder**, tap the **Menu** ☰ icon, tap **Settings**, tap **Reading Options**, then tap **Vocabulary Builder**. While it's turned off, new words won't be added.

Translate Text with Instant Translations

While reading, you can select text, then use **Instant Translations** to see the text in a different language.

1. While reading, press and drag to highlight the text you want to translate.

2. In the pop-up menu, tap **More**, tap **Translation**, and then select the language you want the text translated to.

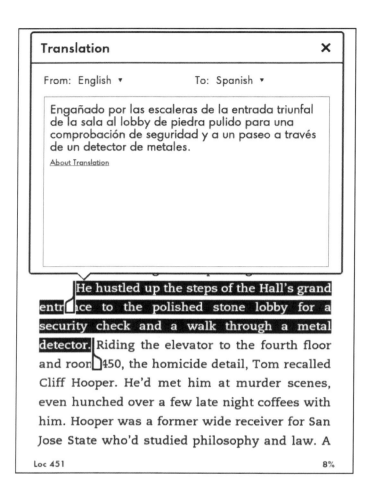

At left: Translating a passage from English to Spanish

Set Up Kindle FreeTime

If you have a young child in the home, consider setting up Kindle FreeTime by setting a Parental Controls password and creating a profile for your child. Kindle FreeTime automatically blocks access to the Kindle store, the web browser, and Wikipedia. Children can only read books you've added to their library.

1. From Home, tap the **Menu** ☰ icon, then tap **Kindle Freetime**.

2. Tap **Get Started**.

3. Enter a password. This password is the same as your Parental Controls password, if you've already created one.

4. Enter your child's name, date of birth, and gender, then tap **Next**. A list of the titles in **Your Kindle Library** appears. (The personal information is used only to tailor the user experience.)

5. Tap the checkbox next to a title to add it to your child's **FreeTime** library, then tap **OK**. (Public library books, personal documents, and books from the Kindle Owner's Lending Library can't be added to a FreeTime profile.)

6. Set your child's **Access to Achievements** and **Daily Reading Goal**. By default, the daily goal is set to 30 minutes.

7. Tap **Finish** to save all settings and create the profile.

Find and Share Books on Goodreads

Goodreads is an online book community owned by Amazon where you can follow friends to see what they're reading, and share and rate books on your Paperwhite.

1. From **Home**, tap the **Goodreads** g icon.

2. Connect your Amazon account to Goodreads using one of these two options:

   • If you already have a Goodreads account, tap **Connect Existing Account**.

   • If you don't already have a Goodreads account, tap **Create New Account**.

3. Tap **+Follow** beside readers you want to follow, then tap **Next**.

4. Add your Amazon books to shelves or rate your books to add them to Goodreads, then tap **Next**. Rate books by tapping the desired numbers of stars next to the book.

Link your Paperwhite to Facebook or Twitter

You can share your reading status, notes, book highlights, and book ratings on Facebook or Twitter. You can link or unlink your device to these social networks at any time.

1. From **Home**, tap the **Menu** ≡ icon, then tap **Settings**.

2. Tap **Reading Options**, then tap **Social Networks**.

3. Tap **Link Account** or **Unlink Account** and follow the on-screen instructions.

Manage Your Subscription Settings

You can make changes to your subscriptions to magazines, newspapers and blogs.

1. Visit **Manage Your Kindle** at www.amazon.com/myk

2. Under **Your Kindle Account**, click **Subscription Settings**.

3. On the **Subscription Settings** page, click the **Actions** button next to the title, then you can:

   • Deliver past issues of subscription content to an eligible Kindle device or app.

   • Cancel a subscription

   • Download a title or issue of a subscription to your computer, then transfer it to your Kindle via USB cable.

- Choose privacy preferences, such as whether to share your email address with subscription publishers.

Edit Device Names

The name of your device is set automatically by Amazon, but you can change the name of the device to make it more meaningful. For example, when my most recent Kindle Paperwhite arrived in its box, Amazon named it "Steve's 6th Kindle." I changed the name to "Steve's New Paperwhite" so that I can distinguish it from my several other Kindle devices purchased earlier.

The device name appears at the upper left corner of your device screen and on the **Manage Your Kindle** page. Here's how to edit the name of your device:

1. Visit **Manage Your Kindle** at www.amazon.com/myk

2. Click **Manage Your Devices**.

3. Click **Edit** beside the name of the device or app.

4. Enter the desired name and click **Update**.

Delete Items From Your Kindle Library

If you want to free up space on your Kindle device, you can tap its icon once, then tap **Remove From Device**. If you wish, you'll be able to send the item to your Kindle at a future point. By contrast, **if you delete an item from your Kindle library, the action is permanent**—you won't be able to download the item again unless you buy it again.

1. Visit **Manage Your Kindle** at www.amazon.com/myk

2. Locate the item you want to delete.

3. From the **Actions** drop-down menu, select **Delete from library**. Confirm by clicking **Yes**.

Index

304 Screen shots

Printed in Great Britain
by Amazon.co.uk, Ltd.,
Marston Gate.